THE ROYAL HORTICULTURAL SOCIETY

WILD IN THE GARDEN

DIARY
2020

First published in 2019 by White Lion Publishing,
an imprint of The Quarto Group.
The Old Brewery, 6 Blundell Street
London, N7 9BH
United Kingdom
T (0)20 7700 6700
www.QuartoKnows.com

RHS FLOWER SHOWS 2020

The Royal Horticultural Society holds a number
of prestigious flower shows throughout the year.
At the time of going to press, show dates for 2020
had not been confirmed but details can be found
on the website at: rhs.org.uk/shows-events

Every effort is made to ensure calendrical data is
correct at the time of going to press but the publisher
cannot accept any liability for any errors or changes.

PICTURE CREDITS

CALENDAR 2020

JANUARY
M	T	W	T	F	S	S
		1	2	3	4	5
6	7	8	9	10	11	12
13	14	15	16	17	18	19
20	21	22	23	24	25	26
27	28	29	30	31		

FEBRUARY
M	T	W	T	F	S	S
					1	2
3	4	5	6	7	8	9
10	11	12	13	14	15	16
17	18	19	20	21	22	23
24	25	26	27	28	29	

MARCH
M	T	W	T	F	S	S
						1
2	3	4	5	6	7	8
9	10	11	12	13	14	15
16	17	18	19	20	21	22
23	24	25	26	27	28	29
30	31					

APRIL
M	T	W	T	F	S	S
		1	2	3	4	5
6	7	8	9	10	11	12
13	14	15	16	17	18	19
20	21	22	23	24	25	26
27	28	29	30			

MAY
M	T	W	T	F	S	S
				1	2	3
4	5	6	7	8	9	10
11	12	13	14	15	16	17
18	19	20	21	22	23	24
25	26	27	28	29	30	31

JUNE
M	T	W	T	F	S	S
1	2	3	4	5	6	7
8	9	10	11	12	13	14
15	16	17	18	19	20	21
22	23	24	25	26	27	28
29	30					

JULY
M	T	W	T	F	S	S
		1	2	3	4	5
6	7	8	9	10	11	12
13	14	15	16	17	18	19
20	21	22	23	24	25	26
27	28	29	30	31		

AUGUST
M	T	W	T	F	S	S
					1	2
3	4	5	6	7	8	9
10	11	12	13	14	15	16
17	18	19	20	21	22	23
24	25	26	27	28	29	30
31						

SEPTEMBER
M	T	W	T	F	S	S
	1	2	3	4	5	6
7	8	9	10	11	12	13
14	15	16	17	18	19	20
21	22	23	24	25	26	27
28	29	30				

OCTOBER
M	T	W	T	F	S	S
			1	2	3	4
5	6	7	8	9	10	11
12	13	14	15	16	17	18
19	20	21	22	23	24	25
26	27	28	29	30	31	

NOVEMBER
M	T	W	T	F	S	S
						1
2	3	4	5	6	7	8
9	10	11	12	13	14	15
16	17	18	19	20	21	22
23	24	25	26	27	28	29
30						

DECEMBER
M	T	W	T	F	S	S
	1	2	3	4	5	6
7	8	9	10	11	12	13
14	15	16	17	18	19	20
21	22	23	24	25	26	27
28	29	30	31			

CALENDAR 2021

JANUARY
M	T	W	T	F	S	S
				1	2	3
4	5	6	7	8	9	10
11	12	13	14	15	16	17
18	19	20	21	22	23	24
25	26	27	28	29	30	31

FEBRUARY
M	T	W	T	F	S	S
1	2	3	4	5	6	7
8	9	10	11	12	13	14
15	16	17	18	19	20	21
22	23	24	25	26	27	28

MARCH
M	T	W	T	F	S	S
1	2	3	4	5	6	7
8	9	10	11	12	13	14
15	16	17	18	19	20	21
22	23	24	25	26	27	28
29	30	31				

APRIL
M	T	W	T	F	S	S
			1	2	3	4
5	6	7	8	9	10	11
12	13	14	15	16	17	18
19	20	21	22	23	24	25
26	27	28	29	30		

MAY
M	T	W	T	F	S	S
					1	2
3	4	5	6	7	8	9
10	11	12	13	14	15	16
17	18	19	20	21	22	23
24	25	26	27	28	29	30
31						

JUNE
M	T	W	T	F	S	S
	1	2	3	4	5	6
7	8	9	10	11	12	13
14	15	16	17	18	19	20
21	22	23	24	25	26	27
28	29	30				

JULY
M	T	W	T	F	S	S
			1	2	3	4
5	6	7	8	9	10	11
12	13	14	15	16	17	18
19	20	21	22	23	24	25
26	27	28	29	30	31	

AUGUST
M	T	W	T	F	S	S
						1
2	3	4	5	6	7	8
9	10	11	12	13	14	15
16	17	18	19	20	21	22
23	24	25	26	27	28	29
30	31					

SEPTEMBER
M	T	W	T	F	S	S
		1	2	3	4	5
6	7	8	9	10	11	12
13	14	15	16	17	18	19
20	21	22	23	24	25	26
27	28	29	30			

OCTOBER
M	T	W	T	F	S	S
				1	2	3
4	5	6	7	8	9	10
11	12	13	14	15	16	17
18	19	20	21	22	23	24
25	26	27	28	29	30	31

NOVEMBER
M	T	W	T	F	S	S
1	2	3	4	5	6	7
8	9	10	11	12	13	14
15	16	17	18	19	20	21
22	23	24	25	26	27	28
29	30					

DECEMBER
M	T	W	T	F	S	S
		1	2	3	4	5
6	7	8	9	10	11	12
13	14	15	16	17	18	19
20	21	22	23	24	25	26
27	28	29	30	31		

GARDENS AND WILDLIFE

Gardens as a network form an important ecosystem. An ecosystem is an interdependent and dynamic system of living organisms which is considered together with the physical and geographical environment. Ecosystems are interdependent because everything in a garden depends on everything else.

The garden ecosystem is extremely variable, thereby offering year-round interest. Gardens offer a large number of animals the perfect conditions for different stages of their life cycle. Insects may prefer sunny, sheltered spots to forage and mate, but their larvae may need to live in water or in rotting vegetation. The large range of garden wildlife is there because of gardening, not despite it.

Due to the nature of gardens, groups of species that exploit a network of gardens' resources can find abundance over a longer time period, compared to what a single natural site can offer. Even gardens that are managed without regard for wildlife still offer some benefit, especially when they are considered as part of the total garden network. Even without simulated 'wild' habitats, gardens are living, diverse ecosystems in their own right. No garden is too small to provide some benefit to wildlife. Many visiting animals can actually be residents of neighbouring gardens. It is the garden network that is of overall importance to wildlife, forming the larger garden ecosystem.

City gardens are important corridors that facilitate the safe movement of birds, butterflies and other wildlife. Wildlife-friendly gardens don't need to be messy, with an abundance of stinging nettles. All gardens offer some resource to certain species, however, with a little thought and planning, every garden can be of great benefit to a much wider range of species. Look around your local area and see what type of habitat is missing and whether it is possible for you to provide it: perhaps a pond, nest-boxes, decaying wood or an undisturbed leaf pile? The more diverse the habitats, the greater the variety of birds and wildlife visiting your garden.

The RHS recognises and actively promotes the valuable contribution that gardens make to wildlife, believing that with thoughtful management it is possible to enhance the wildlife potential in any garden without compromising the gardener's enjoyment of it. For more information visit: **www.rhs.org.uk** and **www.wildaboutgardens.org.uk**

'Check that the water in the bird bath is topped up and not frozen. Despite the cold, many birds still like to bathe.'

JOBS FOR THE MONTH
- Check that the water in the bird bath is topped up and not frozen.
- Put bird food out on the ground and bird table. Hang bird feeders on branches and fences and ensure that they are kept topped up.
- Make sure the pond does not freeze over. To defrost frozen water, fill a saucepan with hot water and rest it on the ice until a hole has melted through.
- Good hygiene is essential to prevent diseases so clean the bird bath and table regularly.

INSECTS
- Bugs and critters are crucial to your garden's ecosystem as not only do they eat your garden pests, they also provide a source of food for birds and small mammals. In many cases they are also important pollinators.
- Plant sea lavender, buddlejas, *Centranthus ruber* and *Lychnis* to encourage day-flying moths.
- Evergreen shrubs provide winter hibernation areas for butterflies and moths.
- Leave areas of the garden, such as tall plants and dense bushes, undisturbed for spiders.

BIRDS
- Thrushes, blackbirds, tits and robins are all common winter birds and following the suggestions below will encourage them to visit your garden.
- Many of the natural food sources for birds are not available in winter so put out bird seed, fat balls and mealworms which will provide necessary fat and protein. Grapes, sultanas, raisins and some artificial sweeteners are toxic to dogs so bear this in mind if you have pets at home.
- You can make your own fat balls using natural fats such as lard and beef suet. Avoid fat from cooking and unsaturated margarines and vegetable oil as these are not suitable.
- Remove old food from the bird table as it can encourage diseases such as salmonella to breed, which can be fatal to birds.
- Don't rush to clear windfall and rotten fruit as these provide food for blackbirds, thrushes and fieldfares.
- Protect birds from predators by siting any bird tables and feeders away from areas easily accessible to cats.
- Do not allow bird droppings to accumulate: always sweep and clean them up.

DECEMBER & JANUARY 2020

Monday 30

Tuesday 31

New Year's Eve

Wednesday 1

New Year's Day
Holiday, UK, Republic of Ireland, USA,
Canada, Australia and New Zealand

Thursday 2

Holiday, Scotland and New Zealand

Friday 3

First quarter

Saturday 4

Sunday 5

JANUARY

6 *Monday*   Epiphany

7 *Tuesday*

8 *Wednesday*

9 *Thursday*

10 *Friday*   Full moon

11 *Saturday*

12 *Sunday*

Great spotted woodpecker (*Dendrocopos major*)

JANUARY

Monday 13

Tuesday 14

Wednesday 15

Thursday 16

st quarter *Friday* 17

Saturday 18

Sunday 19

nesting box hanging on a tree

JANUARY

20 *Monday*

21 *Tuesday*

22 *Wednesday*

23 *Thursday*

24 *Friday* New moo

25 *Saturday* Chinese New Ye

26 *Sunday* Australia Da

Banded demoiselle damselfly *(Calopteryx splendens*

JANUARY & FEBRUARY

oliday, Australia (Australia Day)

Monday 27

Tuesday 28

Wednesday 29

Thursday 30

Friday 31

Saturday 1

First quarter

Sunday 2

Magpie *(Pica pica)*

FEBRUARY

3 *Monday*

4 *Tuesday*

5 *Wednesday*

6 *Thursday*

Accession of Queen Elizabeth
Holiday, New Zealand (Waitangi Da

7 *Friday*

8 *Saturday*

9 *Sunday*

Full moo

*consider building a home
for solitary mason bees
to colonise in the spring.'*

JOBS FOR THE MONTH
- Make sure the bird bath and table are kept clear of snow.
- Put up nesting boxes for birds. Research different types if you want to attract particular species to the garden.
- Put out hedgehog food (dog food is a good substitute).
- Keep bird feeders topped up and continue to put food out on the ground and bird table. Avoid putting out large chunks of food that can be a choking hazard for fledglings.

HABITATS AND SHELTER
- A pile of old logs or bricks or turned-over empty pots can provide welcome shelter for insects and other small creatures.
- Hang nesting boxes on walls rather than trees to protect birds from predators like cats. Tilt the box forward slightly to reduce the splash from rain showers. Sunlight can make a nesting box uninviting so position the box so that it's north or north-east facing.
- Consider building a home for masonry bees to colonise in the spring.

PONDS
- The smallest pond will attract dragonflies, damselflies and other insects, as well as newts, toads and frogs. A pond or water feature is a key water source for all garden wildlife.
- Choose a bright and sunny location with space for planting around the edges to create a corridor to hibernation areas and a food source.
- Late winter is a great time to put in a pond. You may get your first frogs and toads by spring.
- Make sure it's easy to access the water by placing rocks and stones around the edge of the pond. Birds like a large flat rock sitting just beneath the surface for easy drinking and bathing.
- Connect your water butt so that it can fill the pond automatically when it rains.
- Avoid using cobbles and paving around the edges as these surfaces can get very hot and be detrimental to young amphibians.
- Vary the depth of water so there are shallow areas as well as deeper water, which will help some aquatic insects survive cold weather.

FEBRUARY

Monday 10

Tuesday 11

Wednesday 12

Thursday 13

Valentine's Day

Friday 14

Last quarter

Saturday 15

Sunday 16

Elephant hawk moth (*Deilephila elpenor*)

FEBRUARY

17 *Monday*

18 *Tuesday*

19 *Wednesday*

20 *Thursday*

21 *Friday*

22 *Saturday*

23 *Sunday* New moon

Pink lotus *(Nelumbo nucifera)* lily pads in garden pond

FEBRUARY & MARCH

Monday 24

Shrove Tuesday

Tuesday 25

Ash Wednesday

Wednesday 26

Thursday 27

Friday 28

Saturday 29

St David's Day

Sunday 1

Tawny owl *(Strix aluco)*

MARCH

---

2 *Monday*

---

3 *Tuesday*

---

4 *Wednesday*

---

5 *Thursday*

---

6 *Friday*

---

7 *Saturday*

---

8 *Sunday*

Create shelter for wildlife by making log piles using twigs, felled trees and debris for nests.

JOBS FOR THE MONTH
- Hang out bee and bird nesting boxes.
- Remove netting placed over the pond to protect it from autumn leaf fall.
- Make your pond wildlife friendly (see Week 6).
- Top up bird feeders and put out food on surfaces and on the ground.
- Refrain from using chunky foods that might cause young birds to choke.
- Sow or plant a wildflower meadow.

MAMMALS AND AMPHIBIANS
- Frogs, toads and hedgehogs emerge from hibernation as the weather warms up.
- Create shelter for wildlife by making log piles using twigs, felled trees and debris for nests.
- Look out for amphibian spawn in ponds. Frog spawn is usually in jelly-like clumps; toad spawn is in longer individual strands; and newt spawn is laid individually on pondweed stems.

WAYS TO ENCOURAGE WILDLIFE
- Weed by hand as much as possible to avoid using herbicides.
- Build a compost heap to generate insects for bats and other small creatures, as well as a hibernation site.
- Use mulch to deter weeds and also provide insect habitats.
- Plant berry-producing varieties which can provide a good winter food source for local wildlife.
- Allow some of your plants to go to seed.
- Plant native species to support wildlife; honeysuckle, sunflower, hawthorn and rowan trees are all popular with birds.
- Butterflies may emerge during spells of sunshine; look out for Brimstones and Commas.
- Replace a fence with a native hedge to provide a safe, covered path for wildlife as well as a hibernation and nesting site and food source.
- Create a pond or water feature.

MARCH

Monday 9

Tuesday 10

Wednesday 11

Thursday 12

Friday 13

Saturday 14

Sunday 15

Garden spider *(Araneus diadematus)*

MARCH

---

16 *Monday*   *Last quart*

---

17 *Tuesday*   Holiday, Republic of Ireland and Northern Irela
(St Patrick's Da

---

18 *Wednesday*

---

19 *Thursday*

---

20 *Friday*   Vernal Equinox (Spring begin

---

21 *Saturday*

---

22 *Sunday*   Mothering Sunday, UK and Republic of Irelan

Water vole (*Arvicola amphibius*

MARCH

Monday 23

new moon

Tuesday 24

Wednesday 25

Thursday 26

Friday 27

Saturday 28

British Summer Time begins

Sunday 29

Red squirrel *(Sciurus vulgaris)*

MARCH & APRIL

30 *Monday*

31 *Tuesday*

1 *Wednesday* — *First quarter*

2 *Thursday*

3 *Friday*

4 *Saturday*

5 *Sunday*

Blue tit *(Cyanistes caeruleus)*

'Clean your bird feeders and move their placement around the garden regularly to avoid ruining the ground underneath.'

JOBS FOR THE MONTH

- Plant single flowers (rather than doubles) to encourage beneficial insects into the garden.
- Fill up bird feeders and put out additional food on the bird table and ground.
- Clean the feeders regularly and move them around the garden to avoid ruining the ground underneath.
- Build piles of twigs, branches and rocks to create shelter for wildlife.
- Leave out food for hedgehogs.

BATS

- Now is the time that bats begin to nest, so why not make or buy a bat box and hang it on a sunny wall. Other common nesting areas are eaves and behind weatherboarding on the south face of buildings.
- Midges and other garden pests are commonly feasted on by bats so this is a good reason to make your garden more bat friendly.
- Where possible retain old trees with splits or cavities in the branches and trunk.
- Be more accepting of insects. A few caterpillars will not cause too much damage to your garden but will provide a bat with a tasty meal.
- Compost heaps also encourage the types of insects that bats like to eat.
- White or pale-coloured flowers are more visible to nocturnal insects, including moths, which bats regularly feast on.
- Avoid using pesticides if possible.

APRIL

Monday 6

Tuesday 7

Full moon

Wednesday 8

First day of Passover (Pesach)
Maundy Thursday

Thursday 9

Good Friday
Holiday, UK, Canada, Australia and New Zealand

Friday 10

Saturday 11

Easter Sunday

Sunday 12

APRIL

13 *Monday*

Easter Monda
Holiday, UK (exc. Scotland), Republic of Irelan
Australia and New Zealan

14 *Tuesday*

Last quarte

15 *Wednesday*

16 *Thursday*

17 *Friday*

18 *Saturday*

19 *Sunday*

Mole (Talpa europaea,

APRIL

Monday 20

Birthday of Queen Elizabeth II

Tuesday 21

Wednesday 22

New moon
St George's Day

Thursday 23

First day of Ramadân
(subject to sighting of the moon)

Friday 24

Anzac Day

Saturday 25

Sunday 26

European starling *(Sturnus vulgaris)*

APRIL & MAY

27 *Monday*

28 *Tuesday*

29 *Wednesday*

30 *Thursday*

First quart

1 *Friday*

2 *Saturday*

3 *Sunday*

'Hedgehogs are very active at this time of year, looking around for mates and foraging for food.'

JOBS FOR THE MONTH

- Leave informal hedges untrimmed to provide food and shelter for wildlife.
- Plant a mixture of annuals and perennials to appeal to different insects.
- Create log, twig or rock piles to create shelter for wildlife.
- Remove weeds from ponds, taking care to leave them on the side for twenty-four hours to allow trapped creatures to return to the water before adding them to the compost heap.
- Make your pond more wildlife-friendly.
- Be careful not to disturb nesting birds in garden shrubs and hedges.
- Regularly clean and top up the bird bath and table.
- Top up bird feeders and scatter food on the ground. Avoid anything too chunky that might cause young fledglings to choke.
- Put up nesting boxes.

MAMMALS

- Many creatures give birth to their young around this time of the year.
- Hedgehogs are very active in particular, often looking around for mates and foraging for food.
- Don't use more slug pellets than strictly necessary. It is much better to consider ecological and wildlife-friendly alternatives.

BIRDS

- Migrant birds from Africa have arrived.
- Swallows will nest on any suitable ledge or shelf in quiet outbuildings.
- The dawn chorus can be deafening as birds compete with each other for mates.

INSECTS

- Bees are starting to be more common.
- Damselflies and large iridescent dragonflies are attracted to ponds.
- Pond skaters and water boatmen can also be found around water, often on pond surfaces.

MAY

Early Spring Bank Holiday, UK
Holiday, Republic of Ireland

Monday 4

Tuesday 5

Wednesday 6

Full moon

Thursday 7

Friday 8

Saturday 9

Mother's Day, USA, Canada,
Australia and New Zealand

Sunday 10

A female blackbird takes a drink at a bird bath

MAY

---

11 *Monday*

---

12 *Tuesday*

---

13 *Wednesday*

---

14 *Thursday* *Last quarter*

---

15 *Friday*

---

16 *Saturday*

---

17 *Sunday*

Painted lady butterflies *(Vanessa cardu...*

MAY

Holiday, Canada (Victoria Day)

Monday 18

Tuesday 19

Wednesday 20

Ascension Day

Thursday 21

New moon

Friday 22

Eid al-Fitr (end of Ramadān)
(subject to sighting of the moon)

Saturday 23

Sunday 24

Nuthatch *(Sitta europaea)*

MAY

25 *Monday*   Spring Bank Holiday, U
                                                      Holiday, USA (Memorial Day

26 *Tuesday*

27 *Wednesday*

28 *Thursday*

29 *Friday*   Feast of Weeks (Shavuo

30 *Saturday*   *First quarte*

31 *Sunday*   Whit Sunda

A frog sitting on a leaf in a pon

'Put up a bat nesting box to encourange bats into your garden.'

JOBS FOR THE MONTH

- Try not to disturb nesting birds in garden shrubs and hedges.
- Mow spring flowering meadows once bulb foliage has died down.
- Mow recently established perennial meadows to control weeds.
- Use wildlife-friendly pesticides and slug pellets if chemical slug control is required.
- Put up a bat nesting box.
- Put out hedgehog food.
- Top up bird feeders and put food out on the ground and bird tables.
- Avoid chunky foods that choke young fledglings.
- Regularly clean out the bird bath and table to avoid bacteria and salmonella developing.
- Regularly refill the bird table.
- Make the pond more wildlife-friendly (see Week 6).

HOW TO CHOOSE BIRD FOOD

- Bird food doesn't have to be expensive and you can easily make your own. When putting out food, think about different breeds' requirements, especially if you're trying to encourage particular species into your garden.
- **Blackbirds and thrushes:** fruit like over-ripe apples, raisins and songbird mix scattered on the ground
- **Dunnocks:** crumbs of bread and fat and small seed from the ground
- **Finches:** berry cakes
- **Goldfinches:** niger seeds
- **Robins:** live mealworms
- **Sparrows, nuthatches and finches:** sunflower heads
- **Starlings:** peanut cakes
- **Tits:** insect cakes
- **Wrens:** prefer natural foods but will also eat fat, bread and seed if the winter weather is particularly harsh

JUNE

Holiday, Republic of Ireland
Holiday, New Zealand (The Queen's Birthday)

Monday **1**

Coronation Day

Tuesday **2**

Wednesday **3**

Thursday **4**

Full moon

Friday **5**

Saturday **6**

Sunday **7**

JUNE

8 *Monday* — Holiday, Australia (The Queen's Birthda

9 *Tuesday*

10 *Wednesday*

11 *Thursday* — Corpus Christ

12 *Friday*

13 *Saturday* — Last quarte
The Queen's Official Birthda
(subject to confirmation

14 *Sunday*

Grey squirrel *(Sciurus carolinensis*

JUNE

Monday 15

Tuesday 16

Wednesday 17

Thursday 18

Friday 19

Summer Solstice (Summer begins)

Saturday 20

New moon
Father's Day, UK, Republic of Ireland,
USA and Canada

Sunday 21

European Goldfinch *(Carduelis carduelis)*

JUNE

22 *Monday*

23 *Tuesday*

24 *Wednesday*

25 *Thursday*

26 *Friday*

27 *Saturday*

28 *Sunday*
First quarter

A colourful garden border featuring *Lysimachia*, *Lupinus*, *Helenium* and *Leucanthemum*

'Young mammals are starting to venture out of the nest.'

JOBS FOR THE MONTH

- Top up ponds and water features. Use a hose with spray attachment to add oxygen and aerate the water for any fish living in the pond.
- Remove dead foliage and blooms from aquatic plants.
- Avoid deadheading roses that produce hips, as these are an important food source.
- Leave out hedgehog food.
- Build a hedgehog hibernation box for the coming winter.
- Plant annuals and perennials to attract insects. In particular, marigolds placed around the vegetable patch will attract hoverflies which will help with pest control.
- Prune hedges and large bushes less frequently as they are often used for shelter by different garden creatures.
- Leave nesting birds undisturbed in shrubs and trees.
- Clean the bird bath regularly and make sure that it's topped up with fresh water.
- Put food out on the ground and bird table but avoid chunky food that might cause young fledglings to choke.
- Go bat watching in the evening.
- Watch out for adult frogs and toads leaving the pond.

MAMMALS AND AMPHIBIANS

- Young mammals born earlier in the year are now venturing out of the nest. Young litters of hedgehogs are now learning how to survive and may be seen gathering food at night.
- Adult frogs, toads and newts start leaving the pond when the ground is damp. Rocks, logs and leafy plants near and around the pond's edge will offer protection from the sun and predators.
- It is also bat-watching season.

IN THE GARDEN

- Marigolds are traditionally planted around vegetable patches to attract hoverflies which act as natural pest control for the crops.
- Remove dead foliage and blooms from water lilies and other aquatic plants.
- Be tolerant and leave a few spare caterpillars to feed bats and avoid using pesicides where possible.

INSECTS

- Hoverflies are in abundance during summer. They are good for pest control, as are wasps, who like to feast on flies and grubs. They can also be effective pollinators.

JUNE & JULY

Monday 29

Tuesday 30

oliday, Canada (Canada Day)   *Wednesday* 1

Thursday 2

Holiday, USA (Independence Day)   *Friday* 3

ndependence Day   *Saturday* 4

Full moon   *Sunday* 5

JULY

6 *Monday*

7 *Tuesday*

8 *Wednesday*

9 *Thursday*

10 *Friday*

11 *Saturday*

12 *Sunday*

Last quarter
Battle of the Boyne

Wild rabbit *(Oryctolagus cuniculus*

oliday, Northern Ireland
(Battle of the Boyne)

Monday 13

Tuesday 14

Swithin's Day

Wednesday 15

Thursday 16

Friday 17

Saturday 18

Sunday 19

parrow *(Passer domesticus)*

JULY

---

20 *Monday*

---

21 *Tuesday*

---

22 *Wednesday*

---

23 *Thursday*

---

24 *Friday*

---

25 *Saturday*

---

26 *Sunday*

Blackberries *(Rubu*

JULY & AUGUST

Monday 27

Tuesday 28

Wednesday 29

Thursday 30

Friday 31

Saturday 1

Sunday 2

Bumblebee collecting pollen from a thistle flower

AUGUST

3 *Monday*

Full moon
Holiday, Scotland and Republic of Ireland

4 *Tuesday*

5 *Wednesday*

6 *Thursday*

7 *Friday*

8 *Saturday*

9 *Sunday*

'Grey squirrels can be heard chattering and squealing as they chase each other over the tree-tops.'

JOBS FOR THE MONTH

- Allow seed heads to develop on some plants as they are a good food source.
- Plant marigolds around the vegetable plot for pest control.
- Plant annuals and perennials to attract insects.
- Top up bird feeders and put food out on bird tables and scatter it on the ground.
- Avoid chunky foods that can be a choking hazard to young fledglings.
- Keep the bird bath clean and topped up, especially as other sources of water may not be available.
- Try not to disturb nesting birds in garden shrubs and trees.
- Trim hedges less frequently to allow wildlife to shelter and feed in them.
- Build a hedgehog hibernation box.
- Leave out hedgehog food.
- Leave some windfall apples, pears and plums for birds to feed on.

IN THE GARDEN

- Bats can be spotted from bridges at night flying over water whilst hunting for insects.
- August sees the departure of the swifts. The majority of other migrant bird species can still be found in the garden. Starlings, jackdaws and sparrows, in particular, can be seen caring for their young in the nest.
- Grey squirrels can be heard chattering and squealing at one another whilst chasing each other over the tree-tops.
- Young birds can be seen exploring their surroundings.
- Birdsong may be reduced this month.
- If it is hot, you may see birds enjoying a 'dust-bath' as well as the bird bath.
- August marks the beginning of the flying season. Winged ants emerge from their nests and fly into the air to mate.
- New frogs and newts start to leave the ponds where they were born to find new homes.

AUGUST

Monday **10**

Last quarter

Tuesday **11**

Wednesday **12**

Thursday **13**

Friday **14**

Saturday **15**

Sunday **16**

Red fox *(Vulpes vulpes)*

AUGUST

17 *Monday*

18 *Tuesday*

19 *Wednesday*　　　　　　　　　　　　　　　　　*New moon*

20 *Thursday*　　　　　　　　　　　　　　　Islamic New Year

21 *Friday*

22 *Saturday*

23 *Sunday*

Insect hotel made of wood and bamboo sticks

AUGUST

Monday 24

First quarter

Tuesday 25

Wednesday 26

Thursday 27

Friday 28

Saturday 29

Sunday 30

Caterpillar

AUGUST & SEPTEMBER

31 *Monday*   Summer Bank Holiday, UK (exc. Scotland)

---

1 *Tuesday*

---

2 *Wednesday*   Full moon

---

3 *Thursday*

---

4 *Friday*

---

5 *Saturday*

---

6 *Sunday*   Father's Day, Australia and New Zealand

'This is the season for bat watching.'

JOBS FOR THE MONTH

- Cover the pond surface with netting to stop fallen leaves from entering.
- Give meadows a final trim before winter.
- Trim hedges less frequently to create shelter for wildlife. They can also be an important food source.
- Construct a hedgehog hibernation box and put out hedgehog food.
- Continue to feed birds, topping up their feeders and scattering food over the bird tables and the ground.
- Avoid putting out food that is too chunky as it may lead fledglings to choke.
- Make sure the bird bath is regularly topped up.

IN THE GARDEN

- Leave meadow clippings on the ground for a couple of days so that any wildlife living inside it can crawl back to safety.
- Divide waterlilies and other pond plants to keep them healthy.
- Flowers provide pollen and nectar for insects so keep dead-heading them to encourage plants to continue producing into autumn.
- If the evenings are warm, you spot bats flying overhead.

BIRDS

- Migrant birds are beginning to leave the garden and return home.
- Native birds are more visible as their moult is over.
- Bird song is back to its usual summer volume.
- Birds are beginning to develop their winter coats and this process consumes a lot of energy. Leaving out a range of foods in your garden during September can really help this process.

SEPTEMBER

Holiday, USA (Labor Day)
Holiday, Canada (Labour Day)

Monday 7

Tuesday 8

Wednesday 9

last quarter

Thursday 10

Friday 11

Saturday 12

Sunday 13

Chaffinch *(Fringilla coelebs)*

SEPTEMBER

---

14 *Monday*

---

15 *Tuesday*

---

16 *Wednesday*

---

17 *Thursday*   New mo

---

18 *Friday*

---

19 *Saturday*   Jewish New Year (Rosh Hashana

---

20 *Sunday*

A ladybird on an app

SEPTEMBER

Monday **21**

Autumnal Equinox (Autumn begins)

Tuesday **22**

Wednesday **23**

First quarter

Thursday **24**

Friday **25**

Saturday **26**

Sunday **27**

European hedgehog *(Erinceus europaeus)*

SEPTEMBER & OCTOBER

28 *Monday* Day of Atonement (Yom Kippur)

29 *Tuesday* Michaelmas Day

30 *Wednesday*

1 *Thursday* Full moon

2 *Friday*

3 *Saturday* First day of Tabernacles (Succoth)

4 *Sunday*

'Autumn daisies are a good source of food for butterflies and bees.'

JOBS FOR THE MONTH

- Make a leaf pile for hibernating animals and overwintering ground-feeding birds. Include some logs to appeal to insects or build a 'bug hotel'.
- Leave seed heads standing to provide food and shelter for wildlife.
- Where possible, allow uncut ivy to flower as it is an excellent late nectar source for insects.
- Build a hedgehog box and leave out hedgehog food.
- Top up bird feeders and put food out on bird tables and the ground. All feeds, including peanuts, are safe, as the breeding season is now over.
- Clean the bird bath regularly, and make sure it's topped up with fresh water.
- Be careful when turning over compost heaps, as small animals like frogs and toads may be sheltering there.

INSECTS

- Insects need a helping hand to survive the cold weather. A few simple steps will help different species thrive in your garden.
- Leave herbaceous and hollow-stemmed plants unpruned until early spring to provide homes for overwintering insects.
- Plant autumn daisies as these are a good source of food for butterflies and bees, particularly as there are few other plants for them to feed on.
- Whilst caterpillars will eat your plants, they do grow into butterflies that contribute to the garden by helping with pollination. Favourite foods of caterpillars include thistle, stinging nettle, wild carrot, buckthorn and blackthorn.

BIRDS

- You may find your garden feeders are untouched as natural food is in abundance at the moment. Do your bit by making sure your garden is a natural food 'café'.
- Allow your lawn to grow longer and try to avoid chemical sprays. This will allow insect-life to thrive and in turn provide a feeding station for birds.
- Late flowering plants such as Japanese anemones will also provide a food source for birds.

OCTOBER

Monday 5

Tuesday 6

Wednesday 7

Thursday 8

Friday 9

Last quarter

Saturday 10

Sunday 11

OCTOBER

12 *Monday*

13 *Tuesday*

14 *Wednesday*

15 *Thursday*

16 *Friday*   *New moon*

17 *Saturday*

18 *Sunday*

Young kingfisher *(Alcedo atthis)*

OCTOBER

Monday 19

Tuesday 20

Wednesday 21

Thursday 22

First quarter

Friday 23

Saturday 24

British Summer Time ends

Sunday 25

Bullfinch *(Pyrrhula pyrrhula)*

OCTOBER & NOVEMBER

26 *Monday*

Holiday, Republic of Ireland
Holiday, New Zealand (Labour Day)

27 *Tuesday*

28 *Wednesday*

29 *Thursday*

30 *Friday*

31 *Saturday*

Full moon
Halloween

1 *Sunday*

All Saints' Day

Young grey squirrels peering out of their nest

'Make a leaf pile for hibernating creatures and overwintering birds.'

JOBS FOR THE MONTH

- Now that the breeding season is over, all bird feeds are safe so continue to put out food regularly.
- Empty and clean out nesting boxes using boiling water. When the wood has dried out thoroughly, place a handful of wood shavings inside. This will provide winter shelter. Please note: it is illegal to remove unhatched eggs except for between November and January.
- Keep the bird bath topped up and clean regularly.
- Make a hedgehog hibernation box.
- Regularly shake off leaves from nets over ponds. Rake off leaves from ponds that haven't been netted.
- Make a leaf pile for hibernating creatures and overwintering birds that are ground-feeding.
- Leave seed heads standing to provide food and shelter for wildlife.
- Leave mature ivy uncut to flower. The nectar is a good food source for insects.

MOTHS

- There are over 2,500 species of moths in the garden and they play an important role in indicating the health of the garden as they are very sensitive to change.
- Adult moths and their caterpillars are a key food source for various forms of wildlife including hedgehogs, spiders, frogs, bats and birds. Day moths act as plant pollinators whilst feeding on their nectar.
- A decline in moths will have a knock-on effect on predators including bats and cuckoos, who rely on them as a food source.
- Leave longer grasses, thistles and knapweeds in the garden.
- Leave hedges untrimmed if possible.
- Plant evergreen shrubs that will provide winter hibernation sites for butterflies and moths.
- Plant buddlejas, *Centranthus ruber*, *Lychnis* and sea lavender to attract day-flying moths.
- Plant birch, hawthorn, hornbeam, lady's bedstraw, oak and willow to support moth caterpillars.
- Night-flowering, nectar-rich plants and pale-coloured flowering plants will all attract nocturnal moths.

NOVEMBER

Monday 2

Tuesday 3

Wednesday 4

Guy Fawkes

Thursday 5

Friday 6

Saturday 7

last quarter
Remembrance Sunday

Sunday 8

NOVEMBER

9 *Monday*

10 *Tuesday*

11 *Wednesday*

Holiday, USA (Veterans Day)
Holiday, Canada (Remembrance Day)

12 *Thursday*

13 *Friday*

14 *Saturday*

15 *Sunday*

New moon

European nuthatches (*Sitta europae*

NOVEMBER

Monday 16

Tuesday 17

Wednesday 18

Thursday 19

Friday 20

Saturday 21

First quarter

Sunday 22

Harvest mouse *(Micromys minutus)*

NOVEMBER

23 *Monday*

24 *Tuesday*

25 *Wednesday*

26 *Thursday*   Holiday, USA (Thanksgiving)

27 *Friday*

28 *Saturday*

29 *Sunday*   First Sunday in Advent

European crested tit *(Lophophanes cristatus)*

'Plant a single native tree to provide a habitat for those at the bottom of the food chain.'

JOBS FOR THE MONTH
- Keep the bird bath topped up, clean and ice-free.
- Fill up bird feeders and leave food out on bird tables and on the ground. Try to maintain a regular feeding regime, as this will encourage birds to return.
- Because the breeding season is over, all bird feed, including peanuts, are safe to leave out.
- Holly (*Ilex*) is a traditional part of Christmas, however, the holly berries are a valuable food source for birds so think twice before using them in your decorations.
- Leave seed heads standing to provide food and shelter for wildlife.
- If possible leave mature ivy uncut to flower.
- Make a leaf pile for hibernating creatures and overwintering ground-feeding birds.

IN THE GARDEN
Consider planting more shrubs and trees that produce berries as these will provide a valuable food source for birds. Red and orange berries are reported to be more popular with birds than other berries.

PLAN FOR VARYING HABITATS
- Winter is the ideal time to plan your garden if you want to encourage wildlife. Building a range of difficult habitats will support the needs of different creatures across the food chain. Key habitats that you could include are a lawn, trees, shrubs, flowers and water. Consider the habitats that are in the neighbouring gardens: are there any gaps?
- Plant a single native tree to provide a habitat for those at the bottom of the food chain.
- Prune your shrubs at different times to create varied cycles of growth to benefit wildlife.
- Think about planting early- and late-flowering plants to help bridge the lean period before and after summer.
- Create micro-habitats such as small patches of grass to allow birds easy access to grubs and worms. Long grass creates habitats for egg laying and overwintering insects; a pile of logs will provide shelter for small animals.

NOVEMBER & DECEMBER

Full moon
St Andrew's Day

Monday 30

Tuesday 1

Wednesday 2

Thursday 3

Friday 4

Saturday 5

Sunday 6

DECEMBER

7 *Monday*

8 *Tuesday* — *Last quarter*

9 *Wednesday*

10 *Thursday* — Hanukkah begins (at sunset)

11 *Friday*

12 *Saturday*

13 *Sunday*

Hazel dormouse *(Muscardinus avellanarius)*

DECEMBER

Monday **14**

Tuesday **15**

Wednesday **16**

Thursday **17**

Friday **18**

Saturday **19**

Sunday **20**

Roe deer *(Capreolus capreolus)*

DECEMBER

---

21 *Monday*

First quart
Winter Solstice (Winter begin

---

22 *Tuesday*

---

23 *Wednesday*

---

24 *Thursday*

Christmas Ev

---

25 *Friday*

Christmas Da
Holiday, UK, Republic of Ireland, USA
Canada, Australia and New Zealan

---

26 *Saturday*

Boxing Da

---

27 *Sunday*

Robin (*Erithacus rubecula*

DECEMBER & JANUARY 2021

Holiday, UK, Republic of Ireland, USA, Canada,
Australia and New Zealand (Boxing Day)

Monday 28

Tuesday 29

Full moon

Wednesday 30

New Year's Eve

Thursday 31

New Year's Day
Holiday, UK, Republic of Ireland, USA,
Canada, Australia and New Zealand

Friday 1

Saturday 2

Sunday 3

Frosted hawthorn *(Crataegus monogyna)* berries in the garden

YEAR PLANNER

JANUARY	JULY
FEBRUARY	AUGUST
MARCH	SEPTEMBER
APRIL	OCTOBER
MAY	NOVEMBER
JUNE	DECEMBER